BOTANICAL BLISS

| 12 beginner-friendly embroidery patterns with iron-on transfers

Stephanie Carswell

EMBROIDERY MADE EASY

DAVID & CHARLES
—PUBLISHING—

www.davidandcharles.com

A DAVID AND CHARLES BOOK
© David and Charles, Ltd 2025

David and Charles is an imprint of David and Charles, Ltd
Suite A, Tourism House, Pynes Hill, Exeter, EX2 5WS

Text, Designs and Photos © Stephanie Carswell 2025
Layout © David and Charles, Ltd 2025

First published in the UK and USA in 2025

Stephanie Carswell has asserted her right to be identified as author of this work in accordance with the Copyright, Designs and Patents Act, 1988.

All rights reserved. No part of this publication may be reproduced in any form or by any means, electronic or mechanical, by photocopying, recording or otherwise, without prior permission in writing from the publisher.

Readers are permitted to reproduce any of the designs in this book for their personal use and without the prior permission of the publisher. However, the designs in this book are copyright and must not be reproduced for resale.

The author and publisher have made every effort to ensure that all the instructions in the book are accurate and safe, and therefore cannot accept liability for any resulting injury, damage or loss to persons or property, however it may arise.

Names of manufacturers and product ranges are provided for the information of readers, with no intention to infringe copyright or trademarks.

A catalogue record for this book is available from the British Library.

ISBN-13: 9781446315330 paperback

This book has been printed on paper from approved suppliers and made from pulp from sustainable sources.

Printed in China by Hong Kong Graphics for:
David and Charles, Ltd
Suite A, Tourism House, Pynes Hill, Exeter, EX2 5WS

10 9 8 7 6 5 4 3 2 1

Publishing Director: Ame Verso
Managing Editor: Jeni Chown
Editor: Jessica Cropper
Project Editor: Jessie Newton
Designer: Jess Pearson
Pre-press Designer: Susan Reansbury
Illustrations and Photography: Stephanie Carswell
Production Manager: Beverley Richardson

David and Charles publishes high-quality books on a wide range of subjects. For more information visit www.davidandcharles.com.

Share your makes with us on social media using #dandcbooks and follow us on Facebook and Instagram by searching for @dandcbooks.

Layout of the digital edition of this book may vary depending on reader hardware and display settings.

CONTENTS

INTRODUCTION 4
ABOUT THE DESIGNER 5
TOOLS & MATERIALS 6
USING THIS BOOK 7
STITCH GUIDE 9
BLACKTHORN BRAMBLE 12
FIELDS OF PROVENCE 14
FOREST FERNS 16
HIGHLAND HEATHERS 18
JAPANESE GARDEN 20
ROSE GARDEN 22
SEEDHEAD SPRAY 24
SUCCULENTS 26
WILDFLOWER MEADOW 28
WILDWOOD 30
WINTER WALK 32
WINTERTIDE 34
THE TRANSFERS 36

INTRODUCTION

Welcome to *Botanical Bliss*, an *Embroidery Made Easy* book. I'm Stephanie Carswell, and I am thrilled to share this collection of 12 stunning yet simple designs inspired by the enchanting beauty of nature. As an avid embroiderer, I've always found endless inspiration in the delicate intricacies and vibrant colours of the natural world. This book is my way of bringing that beauty to you, with patterns that are not only easy for beginners to stitch but also a joy to create.

Embroidery has been a passion of mine for many years, and it all started with a fascination for the tiny details that make up the natural world. From romantic sprays of wildflowers to the lush greenery of forests and woods, nature's designs are perfect subjects for embroidery. Each pattern in this book captures a piece of that natural wonder, making it accessible for anyone to recreate with just a needle and thread. It has always been more than just a craft for me; it's a form of meditation; a way to unwind and reconnect. In our non-stop world, finding little moments of peace can be challenging, but that's where embroidery comes in! It offers a soothing rhythm, allowing you to switch off and find tranquillity in the simple act of stitching. The benefits of mindful embroidery are huge, from reducing stress and anxiety to improving concentration and nurturing creativity. Sharing the joy of embroidery with as many people as possible is a mission close to my heart. I believe that everyone can benefit from the peaceful, meditative qualities of this craft, regardless of their skill level. *Botanical Bliss* is designed to be your friendly guide on this journey, providing clear, step-by-step instructions and helpful tips to ensure your success. Each project is crafted to be both straightforward and rewarding, making it easy for beginners to create beautiful pieces they can be proud of.

This book is more than just a collection of patterns; it's an invitation to explore the world of embroidery and to bring the beauty of nature into your life. Whether you're looking to add a touch of botanical elegance to your home or to create thoughtful handmade gifts, these designs are perfect for any occasion. With each stitch, you'll find yourself more connected to the calmness and beauty of the natural world.

I hope that *Botanical Bliss* inspires you to pick up your needle and thread and start stitching. May this book bring you as much joy in creating these designs as I had in designing them.

ABOUT THE DESIGNER

Stephanie, the creative force behind Hawthorn Handmade, has been immersed in the world of craft from a very young age. Her childhood was spent with a pencil in hand, doodling on anything she could find, and trying her hand at crafts such as sewing, enamelling, painting, sculpture and weaving. After a brief period in hospitality and event management, she rediscovered her passion for contemporary crafts while working at a local craft centre. This pivotal moment led her to open her own gallery and workshop space in Dorset in 2010, named Hawthorn.

During the quieter days at her gallery, Stephanie taught herself the art of needle felting, which quickly became a cornerstone of her creative journey. Inspired by the beauty of animals and nature, she began selling her intricate wool sculptures with embroidered details at shows and exhibitions across the country and taught numerous workshops, sharing the magic of transforming fluffy wool into beautiful creations. These workshops eventually inspired her to develop her own line of beginner needle-felting kits, leading to the birth of Hawthorn Handmade in 2013. Her first kits were among the very first UK-made needle-felting kits, and they played a significant role in popularising this delightful craft.

Stephanie's enduring love for doodling has been instrumental in the evolution of Hawthorn Handmade. Her hand-drawn embroidery and cross-stitch designs reflect her deep love for the natural world. She finds that the process of embroidery offers significant mindfulness benefits, providing a calming effect that helps to centre the mind and improve mental health. Over the years, Hawthorn Handmade has become one of the UK's best-known craft companies and has sold over half a million kits, teaching thousands the wonderful craft of embroidery and spreading the joy and therapeutic benefits of this art form.

Website: hawthornhandmade.com
- @hawthornhandmade
- /hawthornhandmade
- /hawthornhandmade

TOOLS & MATERIALS

FABRIC

You can embroider on almost any fabric, but for working in a hoop and making a piece you're going to frame, I would always recommend a 100% cotton in a plain weave – that means that the fabric doesn't have too much texture which would otherwise make the stitching difficult. Fabric is often measured in weight, and something around 150-170 gsm (grams per square metre) is ideal. Depending on the colours you choose to use, you could stitch on a coloured fabric rather than just plain white – get creative and have fun with it! You could also choose to transfer the design onto a tote bag, or a jacket or top to embellish it.

TRANSFERS

You can find the transfers for each of the designs in this book from page 37 onwards. There are two ways you can transfer the designs to your fabric, and both are outlined in Using the Transfers on page 11.

HOOP

A good quality hoop makes embroidery so much easier! You ideally want to find a solid wooden hoop which holds its shape well and doesn't easily bend. I would recommend avoiding the cheaper bamboo hoops if your budget allows. Higher quality wooden hoops will grip the fabric better, meaning it will stay taut whilst stitching and won't bend and twist as you work. All the designs in this book use a 7-inch hoop.

THREAD

We have given the colours for DMC threads, but any stranded cotton embroidery thread (floss) or pearl cotton will work. For stranded cotton, I recommend using three strands at a time, but you can change this up for a finer or chunkier look, using fewer or more strands at a time. Some of the designs feature small details where you will need to be using three strands or fewer.

NEEDLE

You will need a 'sharp' embroidery needle for this type of stitching. Look for a dedicated embroidery needle with a larger eye for threading the floss. A size 9 is a good starting place, but maybe get a mixed set so you can try a few sizes and see what you prefer.

EXTRAS

Needle Minders: This is a handy magnetic tool that sits on your fabric and holds on to your needles whilst you're not working.

Needle Threader: A lot of threaders don't work very well when using stranded cotton (floss) and small embroidery needles, but you may find one you like for the needle you have chosen. If you don't have a threader and are struggling, try threading a single strand at a time.

Good Lighting: Embroidery is so much easier with good light! If you're stitching at night or in the winter months, invest in a good LED lamp to give you year round stitching and save your eyes.

USING THIS BOOK

USING THE STITCH KEYS

Each design in this book contains a Stitch Key along with an accompanying diagram to show you where each stitch in the design goes. Matching the colour code in the key to the area drawn in the same colour on the diagram will show you what stitch to use. It's important to remember that this diagram is not to show you which colours go where. Instead, use the DMC Thread Key on each project page along with the photograph on the opposite page to show you where each shade goes.

PUTTING FABRIC IN THE HOOP

Take your hoop and loosen the screw at the top until you can remove the inner ring. Then, place this inner ring on a flat surface and place your fabric on top, centring the design. Now you can place your outer ring over your fabric and push the two into place. Tighten the screw a little and slowly and carefully pull at the edges of your fabric to make it nice and taut in your hoop, taking care not to warp the design. Once your fabric is as tight as a drum, you can now tighten the screw up all the way.

STARTING A STITCH

There are a few ways to start a stitch, and it's all about finding the method you like the most! The easiest way is simply to create a small knot at the end of your thread, and this works well for a lot of projects; however, if you're creating a functional piece, such as a cushion or a quilt, or if you're planning on framing your piece so that it needs to lie flat on a background, you're going to want to use one of the following two methods.

RUN IN (A)

This is a great method for when you already have some existing stitches to work with. With a knot at the end of your thread, weave the needle under approx. 3cm (1⅛in) worth of previous stitches at the back of your design to your next starting point. Take the needle through to the front and work a few stitches before cutting off the knot at the back.

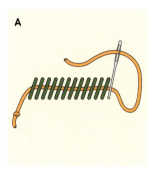

WASTE KNOT (B)

Start with a knot at the end of your thread and stitch through from the front to the back, approx. 3cm (1⅛in) from your starting point, so that the knot sits on the front of your fabric. Start stitching, working towards the waste knot ensuring each stitch secures the thread on the back. When you reach the knot, snip it off and carry on stitching.

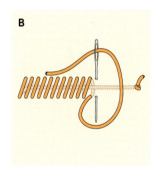

FINISHING A STITCH

Once you've finished a section of your design or come to the end of your thread, bring your needle through to the back of your fabric and weave the thread through a few of the stitches in your design and cut off any excess left over.

USING THE TRANSFERS

There are two ways to use the transfers in this book and it's totally up to you which one you choose. The iron-on method will give you a super accurate outline to follow with your stitches, and the trace-on method will mean you can use your transfer over and over again!

IRON-ON METHOD

Transfer the patterns provided at the back of this book with just a few simple steps.

1. Once you've decided which project you would like to stitch first, gently tear along the perforated edge of your transfer to remove it from the book. Trim the excess paper around the design, leaving an approx. 2.5cm (1in) border. Then, with a dry iron that has the steam setting turned off, press your fabric to make it nice and smooth, ready for the transfer.

3. Next, place the transfer paper onto the fabric with the ink side facing down, and with the iron on its hottest setting, apply it to the top of the transfer, keeping it absolutely still to ensure the ink doesn't bleed, for approximately 45 seconds.

4. Remove the iron and carefully peel back the corner of the paper to check that the design has transferred as it should – be mindful of the hot paper and fabric as you do this!

5. Once the design has been completely transferred and you have removed the transfer paper and allowed the fabric to cool, you can now place the fabric in your hoop and start stitching!

TRACE-ON METHOD (A)

Before you start this method, you'll need a light source and a pencil or a heat or water erasable pen.

1. Remove the transfer from the book by carefully tearing along the perforated edge. Now turn the design over and place it in front of a light source – this can be a window on a sunny day, a light-box or a large device with the brightness turned up – and tape it in place. Position your hoop with the fabric already in it with the fabric sitting flush to the design, with the pattern lined up nice and central.

2. Trace the pattern onto the fabric with a pencil or a heat or water erasable pen. Then, once you have finished tracing your design, remove the fabric from the hoop and reload it into the hoop so that the pattern remains the correct way around. If you have used a heat or water erasable pen, once your stitching is complete, you can remove your marks following the manufacturer's instructions.

FINISHING THE HOOP (B)

To frame your finished embroidery in the hoop, cut off any excess fabric leaving about 1 inch around the edge. Take a length of spare thread one and a half times the length of the circumference, and sew a wide running stitch around the edge of the excess fabric. Once you come back to the first stitch, pull the thread firmly to gather the excess at the back of the hoop. Tie the threads off and trim.

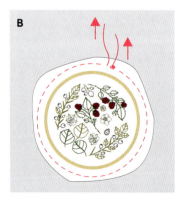

STITCH GUIDE

BACKSTITCH (A)

Start by bringing your needle up through your fabric at the start of your line or shape at point 1. Then, take your needle back down a short distance away at point 2 to make your initial stitch. Bring your needle back up through your fabric at point 3, the same distance away as point 1 is from point 2. Then, stitch back down at point 2 – this is your first backstitch! Continue by bringing your needle up again at point 4, then stitch back down at point 3. Continue on like this until you have completed all your backstitches.

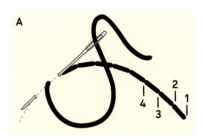

BLANKET STITCH (B)

Imagine you are working along two parallel lines for this stitch – it may help to mark out these lines with an erasable pen. Bring your needle up through your fabric at point 1 to start. Now, take your needle down through the fabric at point 2, diagonally across and up from point 1, on the opposite line, but don't pull your thread taut yet. Instead, bring your needle back up at point 3, catching the loose thread made with that last stitch. You can now pull your thread taut to create a small, backwards 'L' shape. Continue with this pattern until the end of your section.

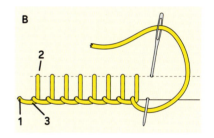

FRENCH KNOT (C)

Bring your needle up through your fabric where you want your French Knot to sit. Next, wrap your thread around your needle twice, keeping the thread taut with your non-working hand (1). Stitch back down immediately next to where you first came up and slowly pull the thread through (2), still keeping it taut, until it's mostly all the way through, then you can let go and allow your newly formed French Knot to sit neatly on top of your fabric (3).

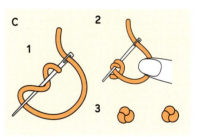

LAZY DAISY (D)

To begin, bring your needle up at point 1. Then, take it back down at point 2, immediately next to it, but don't pull your thread all the way through – instead, leave a little loop. Now, catch that loop of thread by stitching back up at point 3. Finally, anchor it to the top of your fabric by stitching back down at point 4. Once you've mastered this, you can make little lazy daisy flowers by continuing this pattern.

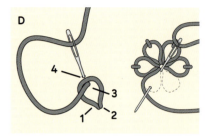

REVERSE CHAIN STITCH (E)

To start, bring your needle up at point 1, then, stitch back down at point 2 to create one small stitch. Then, bring your needle back up at point 3 and carefully thread it under that first stitch keeping the needle and thread on top of the fabric, before stitching back down at point 4, creating a loop. Now, stitch back up at point 5 and thread your needle under the bottom of that last loop before stitching down again at point 6, creating another loop. Continue on like this until the end of your section.

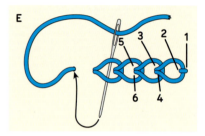

RUNNING STITCH (F)

Bring the needle up through your fabric at point 1. Then, take it back down at point 2, a short distance away. Now, come back up at point 3. Repeat these steps until the end of your section, making sure that all of the gaps between your stitches are of even length.

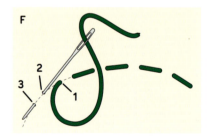

SATIN STITCH (G)

To start, stitch up through your fabric at point 1. Then, take your needle back down at point 2. Next, bring your needle back up at point 3, directly adjacent to point 1, and stitch back down at point 4, directly adjacent to point 2. Continue like this until you have completely filled in your shape, keeping your tension even and filling in any gaps you may accidentally leave as you go along. For complex or curved shapes, you can adjust the angle and length of your stitches to create neat curves and corners.

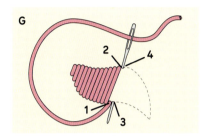

STAR STITCH (H)

Start with a vertical stitch by bringing your needle up at point 1. Then, stitch back down at what will be the centre of your star – point 2. Bring your needle up again at point 3, then back down again at point 2, before stitching back up at point 4. Repeat this until you have completed all of the prongs of your star.

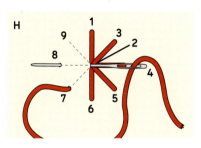

STEM STITCH (I)

Start by bringing your needle up at point 1. Then, stitch back down through your fabric at point 2, but don't pull your thread taut yet and hold it gently out of the way either above or below the line. Now, bring your needle back up at point 3, half way between points 1 and 2, before pulling your thread all the way through. Stitch down at point 4, without pulling your thread taut, and start the process all over again with point 5. Be sure to always hold the loose thread the same side (above or below) for each stitch to get the rope effect.

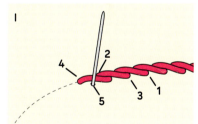

STRAIGHT STITCH (J)

Bring your needle up through your fabric at point 1, then stitch back down at point 2. Repeat this process until you have all the straight stitches you need – if you are filling a section with small, scattered straight stitches, pay extra attention to your tension as you go along so as not to warp your fabric.

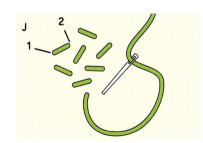

BLACKTHORN BRAMBLE

DMC THREAD KEY

Refer to the photo opposite. Use 3 strands.

- 29
- 522
- 580
- 986
- 915

STITCH KEY

Refer to the diagram (left) and to the Stitch Guide.

- BACKSTITCH
- FRENCH KNOT
- REVERSE CHAIN STITCH
- STEM STITCH
- STRAIGHT STITCH

FIELDS OF PROVENCE

DMC THREAD KEY

Refer to the photo opposite. Use 3 strands.

- 29
- 367
- 725
- 815
- 817
- 3818
- 3836

STITCH KEY

Refer to the diagram (left) and to the Stitch Guide.

- BACKSTITCH
- FRENCH KNOT
- LAZY DAISY
- REVERSE CHAIN STITCH
- SATIN STITCH
- STEM STITCH

FOREST FERNS

DMC THREAD KEY

Refer to the photo opposite.
Use 3 strands.

- 165
- 522
- 580
- 703
- 986

STITCH KEY

Refer to the diagram (left) and to the Stitch Guide.

- BACKSTITCH
- FRENCH KNOT
- REVERSE CHAIN STITCH
- STEM STITCH
- STRAIGHT STITCH

HIGHLAND HEATHERS

DMC THREAD KEY

Refer to the photo opposite. Use 3 strands.

- 18
- 29
- 522
- 535
- 580
- 915

STITCH KEY

Refer to the diagram (left) and to the Stitch Guide.

- BACKSTITCH
- FRENCH KNOT
- LAZY DAISY
- REVERSE CHAIN STITCH
- STRAIGHT STITCH

JAPANESE GARDEN

DMC THREAD KEY

Refer to the photo opposite. Use 3 strands.

- 18
- 522
- 535
- 703
- 3836

STITCH KEY

Refer to the diagram (left) and to the Stitch Guide.

- BACKSTITCH
- FRENCH KNOT
- STEM STITCH

ROSE GARDEN

DMC THREAD KEY

Refer to the photo opposite.
Use 3 strands.

- 29
- 522
- 703
- 815
- 986

STITCH KEY

Refer to the diagram (left) and to the Stitch Guide.

- BACKSTITCH
- BLANKET STITCH
- FRENCH KNOT
- LAZY DAISY
- REVERSE CHAIN STITCH
- SATIN STITCH
- STEM STITCH
- STRAIGHT STITCH

SEEDHEAD SPRAY

DMC THREAD KEY

Refer to the photo opposite.
Use 3 strands.

- 522
- 580
- 703
- 815
- 3836

STITCH KEY

Refer to the diagram (left) and to the Stitch Guide.

- BACKSTITCH
- FRENCH KNOT
- REVERSE CHAIN STITCH
- SATIN STITCH
- STRAIGHT STITCH
- STEM STITCH

SUCCULENTS

DMC THREAD KEY

Refer to the photo opposite.
Use 3 strands.

- 28
- 522
- 580
- 986
- 3810

STITCH KEY

Refer to the diagram (left) and to the Stitch Guide.

- BACKSTITCH
- LAZY DAISY
- REVERSE CHAIN STITCH
- RUNNING STITCH
- STEM STITCH
- STRAIGHT STITCH

Note: where there are thicker black lines shown on two of the succulents, stitch two lines of backstitch side by side

WILDFLOWER MEADOW

DMC THREAD KEY

Refer to the photo opposite.
Use 3 strands.

- 18
- 29
- 522
- 986
- 3836

STITCH KEY

Refer to the diagram (left) and to the Stitch Guide.

- BACKSTITCH
- BLANKET STITCH
- FRENCH KNOT
- REVERSE CHAIN STITCH
- SATIN STITCH
- STEM STITCH

WILDWOOD

DMC THREAD KEY

Refer to the photo opposite. Use 3 strands.

- 18
- 28
- 522
- 580
- 815

STITCH KEY

Refer to the diagram (left) and to the Stitch Guide.

- BACKSTITCH
- FRENCH KNOT
- LAZY DAISY
- SATIN STITCH
- STEM STITCH
- STRAIGHT STITCH

WINTER WALK

DMC THREAD KEY

Refer to the photo opposite.
Use 3 strands.

- 18
- 522
- 580
- 815
- 986

STITCH KEY

Refer to the diagram (left) and to the Stitch Guide.

- BACKSTITCH
- FRENCH KNOT
- REVERSE CHAIN STITCH
- SATIN STITCH
- STAR STITCH
- STEM STITCH
- STRAIGHT STITCH

34

WINTERTIDE

DMC THREAD KEY

Refer to the photo opposite. Use 3 strands.

- 522
- 562
- 730
- 930
- 986

STITCH KEY

Refer to the diagram (left) and to the Stitch Guide.

- BACKSTITCH
- FRENCH KNOT
- REVERSE CHAIN STITCH
- SATIN STITCH
- STEM STITCH

THE TRANSFERS

Here are the 12 easy-to-use transfers to make all of the designs in this book. For instructions on how to use them, turn to page 8 – we've got two different methods to suit your needs. Remember, if you plan to iron your transfer onto your fabric, make sure to do so with the ink side facing down. Happy stitching!

EMBROIDERY MADE EASY